YOU ARE
NOT YOUR
thoughts

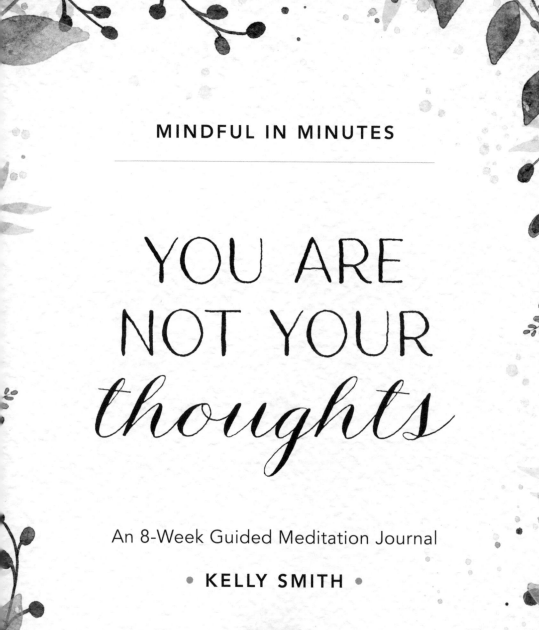

MINDFUL IN MINUTES

YOU ARE
NOT YOUR
thoughts

An 8-Week Guided Meditation Journal

● **KELLY SMITH** ●

FAIR WINDS

Dedication

TO MY PODCAST
LISTENERS. THANK
YOU FOR LETTING
ME BE A PART OF
YOUR LIFE AND FOR
CHANGING MINE.

Introduction

I WANT TO BEGIN THIS JOURNAL BY WELCOMING YOU WITH OPEN ARMS. ANXIETY IS NOT FUN, IT IS NOT EASY, AND IT ISN'T SOMETHING ANY OF US WANT TO LIVE WITH. YET HERE YOU ARE.

Even with whatever you are experiencing right now, you are showing up. You are not alone. Anxiety can feel very different for everyone, but whatever you are feeling and experiencing is valid and real. I welcome you, I respect you, and I hope you give yourself credit for taking this step, as the first step is always the hardest.

By picking up this journal you are choosing to say yes to learning how to soothe your anxious mind, body, and heart through the artful practices of meditation and journaling. You are taking a step toward relief and accepting an invitation to a more mindful and peaceful existence. I couldn't be happier that you are here!

I first dipped my toe into the nervous waters of full-blown anxiety when I was in middle school. I didn't know it at the time, but the sweating, the repetitive thoughts, and the fast heart rate every time someone would talk to me were symptoms of anxiety, and they had come to stay for the long haul. Throughout my life, anxiety has ebbed and flowed through different seasons. It turned me into a person I hardly recognized when it peaked in my early twenties.

But then I discovered meditation, and for the first time in a long time, I felt able to take a full, deep breath. Meditation provided a life raft that not only saved me from drowning in my thoughts, but helped me learn to ride the waves of anxiety as they came. I found that the more I incorporated meditation into my life, the smaller the waves became. I was finally able to live a full, balanced life again.

Over the past ten years, meditation has taught me how to break free from my cycles of anxious thoughts. I've learned how to be an objective observer of what's happening within and around me by cultivating the skill of introspection. Through meditation, I was able to recognize that I was independent from my thoughts—that I existed outside of the inner dialogue that was constantly running in the background of my mind. Like a child holding a balloon, there was the person (me) and then there was the thing I was holding on to (my anxious thoughts). All I had to do was let go and watch that balloon float away into the ether.

Thoughts are just that: thoughts. Not facts, not truths, not certainties. They are as temporary and erratic as that balloon and they exist separately from the person you are at your core. My meditation practice taught me how to exist outside of the anxious background chatter that constantly ran through my mind. I hope this journal will do the same for you.

That's why this journal is titled *You Are Not Your Thoughts*. My hope is that through the next eight weeks, you too will cultivate the skill of introspection— to recognize and release the harmful, debilitating thoughts you're holding onto. This will give you the space and freedom to exist separate from your anxious mind and recognize that anxiety is something that happens to you, it is not you.

Although the gift of introspection and perspective was one of the greatest gifts my meditation practice gave me, it also gave birth to a deep love of writing and creating. Putting pen to paper gave me an outlet to express what I was experiencing through words and visual expression, aiding in my quest to process and release my anxious thoughts. Combining these two habits together in a daily practice gave rise to one of the largest shifts in my relationship with anxiety. Now, I share that practice with you, so that you too can find the peace of mind and freedom you deserve.

For the past ten years, I have shared meditations and practices, just like the ones found in this journal, with my students through classes, workshops, on my podcasts *Mindful in Minutes* and *Meditation Mama*, and on retreats across the globe. To say meditation changed my life would be an understatement; it has transformed my life. And it can transform yours too.

Thanks for being here,

Kelly

HOW TO USE THIS JOURNAL

This journal was designed to help you identify, acknowledge, and explore your anxiety over a period of eight weeks, ultimately leading you to a place of inner calm from which you can manage your anxiety long-term. At the same time, we will be building a foundational and sustainable daily meditation and journaling practice.

If you have the time, I encourage you to read the introductory information at the beginning of this journal. It will help you gain more knowledge about meditation, journaling, and the science behind these practices that proves them to be efficient anxiety fighters. This will help set you up for success in the rest of the program. But if you opened this journal ready to start meditating immediately, feel free to do that as well and return to the introductory section when you're ready for it.

This journal is designed to give you a unique meditation practice, journaling prompt, and mantra each day. Each daily session should take twenty minutes or less. The first week of exercises is designed to help you acknowledge and name your anxiety, as well as receive clarity on the underlying thoughts/feelings/experiences that are contributing to your anxiety.

Then, weeks two through four will focus on the three areas where anxiety manifests itself: your body, mind, and heart. We'll work through each of those areas one at a time, learning unique tools for soothing each one accordingly.

Weeks four through seven will focus on reframing your anxiety, separating yourself from your thoughts, and learning how to move through anxious moments and live with them in a way that feels manageable.

Finally, week eight is a victory lap of sorts. In that week, we will be putting everything together to develop a clear strategy to tackle your anxiety as a whole. At this point, you should feel some relief and see meaningful changes in your relationship with your anxious self.

Each meditation in this book also includes a QR code in the bottom left-hand corner, which, when scanned, will link to an audio recording of that day's meditation, read by me. This is purely a bonus for those readers who prefer to listen in real time to a guided meditation as opposed to reading it.

Because each week builds on the previous weeks' lessons, this journal is most effective when it's done in order from week one to eight. I strongly encourage you to begin on day one and work through this journal every day for a full eight weeks. It takes just twenty minutes a day to do the practice and complete the journal prompt, while the mantra can be used throughout the day and beyond. If you need to skip a day, that's okay. That's life. But I encourage you to try not to skip more than one day. Remember that each day you show up and do the work, you're building a mindful micro-habit that will last you the rest of your life and bring you one step closer to your goal of living anxiety-free.

QUICK-START MEDITATION GUIDE

What is Meditation?

Plain and simple, meditation is the act of single-pointed concentration. It is the ability to completely focus on a single thing for a finite period.

If this sounds like a simple explanation to you, that's good! Meditation is a very simple practice at its core. It isn't complicated, doesn't require a lot of time or props, and can be done anywhere, at any time. I assure you it can be made to fit into a busy lifestyle, no matter how chaotic life feels some days.

Think of meditation like this: Your mind is a light bulb. When you are walking around, experiencing your daily life, your mind's light is on, shining in all directions, illuminating everything around you. But when you sit down to meditate, that light bulb turns into a laser where all that light energy is focused on one point, illuminating only your point of concentration and nothing else.

The point of concentration can vary from practice to practice. For instance, your breath, a mantra, a feeling, or even the words of a guide who is leading a visualization—like you can hear on my podcasts—can all be considered points of concentration. Throughout the next eight weeks, we will be exploring many different points of concentration in our anxiety-easing meditation practices.

Meditation vs. Mindfulness

Throughout this journal, you will be meditating daily and incorporating mindfulness into your life. Although the terms are often used interchangeably, meditation and mindfulness are not the same thing. However, they are related. Think of them as cousins, not twins. While meditation is the act of single-pointed concentration, mindfulness is doing any action or activity with your full attention and awareness. So, if meditation is taking your mental light bulb and turning it into a laser, mindfulness is turning the light bulb up as bright as possible and letting it fully illuminate what is in front of you.

Working through your anxiety and learning how to soothe your anxious mind is usually best mastered through a combination of daily meditation and mindfulness, which is exactly what you will find within the pages of this journal over the next eight weeks.

Meditation Positions

Contrary to common belief, you do not need to sit cross-legged on the floor to meditate. You can meditate anywhere and in any way that you find comfortable. When deciding on your ideal meditation position, you will want to consider the following:

- Can you get comfortable enough that you won't become distracted by unnecessary aches and pains in your body, but not so comfortable that you may fall asleep?

- Can you breathe comfortably without anything interfering with your diaphragm?

- Can you create a long spine in this position, and soften your shoulders?

If you can get comfortable in a position that checks off all these boxes, then well done! You've found a great meditation position. Try your best not to overthink it, but let your body guide you into whichever position is most comfortable each day.

A few alternatives to sitting on the floor are:

- Sitting in a chair with your feet firmly planted on the ground

- Laying down on a yoga mat or in bed

- Sitting on a meditation cushion

- Kneeling on a cushion

- Sitting up in bed with your back resting against the headboard or wall

What to Do with Distractions

Distractions during meditation can come in many forms: intrusive thoughts, itches, worries, external sounds, the urge to move, wondering if you remembered to unplug your curling iron that morning, or constantly thinking about the next item on your to-do list.

Although distractions get a bad rap, I want to propose the radical idea that they are a good thing. They are an important part of the meditation process. If you aren't distracted, then what is the point of meditation? You need distractions to strengthen your mind and build your ability to focus and concentrate, even when your thoughts are wandering.

You can't stop your mind from thinking, just like you can't stop your heart from beating or your hair from growing. It is going to happen. The point of meditation isn't to remove all distractions, but to improve your ability to come back when you inevitably get distracted. Maybe you will begin by getting distracted once every few seconds, but eventually, you will start to become distracted only once every ten seconds, or even once every thirty seconds. Distractions will happen, but it's what you do when they happen that is the true test of your meditation practice. So, accept the distractions, embrace the challenge, and welcome the anxious thoughts without attachment or judgment.

The Anatomy of Anxiety

I have always found comfort in learning the science behind feelings and experiences. For me, understanding the *why* behind something makes it less overwhelming—something I can take small steps toward changing.

When I first learned about the anatomy of anxiety, it allowed me to step outside of what I was experiencing at the moment. I was able to pinpoint what was happening on a physical and neurological level and manage that particular response within my body.

When we look at the anatomy of anxiety, there are three key players: the limbic system, the sympathetic nervous system, and the parasympathetic nervous system.

The limbic system is a key area of the brain for the regulation of emotions, including anxiety. It is responsible for processing incoming stimuli and regulating our emotional responses to those stimuli. The limbic system is made up of key brain regions like the amygdala, hippocampus, and thalamus.

The sympathetic nervous system is often referred to as the "fight-or-flight" mechanism. The main function of the nervous system is to increase blood pressure, produce sweat, dilate blood vessels, and increase the heart rate in response to a trigger, which is what causes that feeling of stress and breathlessness during an anxiety attack.

On the flip side, the parasympathetic nervous system is a network of nerves and mechanisms that relax your body after periods of stress or danger, often referred to as the "rest-and-digest" system. The parasympathetic nervous system helps to bring the body back to a calm and composed state and reduces feelings of stress and anxiety.

When we look at anxiety on a physiological level, these three key players work together in a sort of chain reaction of trigger, interpretation, reaction, and restoration. When you first see a stressor, whether it's a bear crossing your path during a hike, getting a distressing email at work, or even seeing something upsetting on the news, the limbic system will process that stressor, and decide how you should react.

Since our limbic system can't differentiate between different triggers, it will process the bear, email, and news the same way. It will recognize the trigger as a stressor and immediately activate the fight-or-flight mechanism of our sympathetic nervous system as a way of dealing with the potential threat. This causes the elevated heart rate, increased breathing, and sweat that is familiar to all of us as an anxiety attack.

When we are constantly inundated with stressors from various parts of our lives, we can find ourselves living in a constant state of fight-or-flight. Over time, this can have long-lasting negative effects, including increased mass in the amygdala, larger and faster physiological responses to anxiety triggers, and a weakened immune system. Our body adjusts to the prolonged stress, and it makes the stress responses come faster and harder over time to adapt.

To combat this chain reaction of stressor, activation, anxiety, repeat, you must consciously engage in practices to quiet the sympathetic nervous system, so the parasympathetic nervous system can do its work. When the parasympathetic nervous system is working, it quiets the fight-or-flight reaction, lowers your heart rate and respiratory rate, and gives your body time to recoup, rest, and digest, therefore slowing down or stopping those feelings of anxiety.

Some of the most effective ways to quiet the sympathetic nervous system and activate the parasympathetic nervous system are deep breathing, gentle yoga, walks outside, taking breaks from electronic devices, and, you guessed it, meditating and journaling.

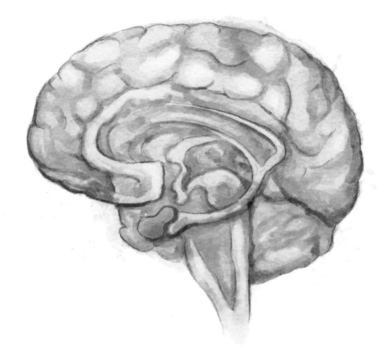

Meditation + Your Brain

We know that anxiety begins with the brain, or more specifically, the limbic system. Now, let's explore how meditation can not only prevent anxiety from happening, but in some cases, reverse the overactivation of the areas of the brain responsible for causing your physiological anxiety symptoms.

Your brain is constantly changing and evolving based on your environment. This is called neuroplasticity and it is a very good thing. It means you aren't doomed to be stuck with your anxious brain forever. Research suggests that just a few small shifts in daily habits—such as adding ten minutes of meditation every day—can change the brain enough to reverse the long-term effects of anxiety. The key players in this process are the amygdala and the prefrontal cortex.

The amygdala is the drama queen of your brain. It is a small almond-shaped region of the brain that plays major roles in pain, fear, worry, and anxiety, as well as your fight-or-flight reaction. In many people suffering from anxiety, the amygdala is larger and overactive compared to those who don't report issues with anxiety.

The prefrontal cortex is responsible for regulating thoughts, actions, and emotions. It helps to predict the consequences of one's actions and to anticipate events in the environment. This means that if, for example, you are someone who gets anxious when talking on the phone, whenever the phone rings or if you even think about the phone ringing, your prefrontal cortex will try to anticipate your emotional reaction, potentially kicking off an anxiety response. It has been shown that this part of the brain can be underactive or smaller in those who are suffering from anxiety, which in some instances can lead to large emotional responses, a decreased ability to focus, or problems with decision-making.

In 2011, Sarah Lazar, Ph.D., a Harvard professor and a pioneer in the study of meditation and the brain, found that regular meditation changes the size of these key regions. In this study, she discovered that over time, usually after about eight weeks of regular meditation, the amygdala began to shrink, while the prefrontal cortex grew in mass and density. In other words, with eight weeks of consistent meditation, your brain can be rewired for smaller anxiety responses and fight or flight reactions, while gaining a greater ability to regulate emotions and focus. Astonishingly, the benefits occurred with just ten minutes of meditation a day, which you are going to replicate with this eight-week journal.

So, the goal here is two-fold. First, to help learn how to soothe the sympathetic nervous system and activate the parasympathetic system to reduce everyday occurrences of anxiety. Second, to begin to reverse some of the negative long-term effects living with anxiety has had on your brain, by simply adding ten minutes of meditation to your day for the next eight weeks.

JOURNALING 101

The concept of journaling is quite simple: It is a written record of your thoughts and feelings. If that definition makes it seem easy, that's because it is! Journaling is a great way of connecting with what is happening in your body, mind, and heart by tracking what is going on in your day-to-day life. Journaling doesn't have a lot of rules. It's an uncomplicated way to meaningfully connect with yourself on a daily basis.

Like meditation, journaling gives a window into what is happening underneath the surface, bringing clarity to your thoughts and feelings. But what makes journaling such a great companion to mindfulness practices is that it provides a record. In your journal, you can track your progress day-to-day and read back through previous entries to look for changes and improvements in your thoughts and emotions over time.

Benefits of Journaling

Journaling has been shown to have great benefits for your mental and emotional health, including:

- Reducing your stress
- Offering a way to identify and track negative thoughts and behaviors
- Clarifying thoughts
- Deepening a connection with the self
- Gaining a new perspective on life
- Helping cope with fearful and sad thoughts
- Reducing instances of overthinking or dwelling on upsetting or worrisome thoughts

There have been several studies conducted on the benefits of journaling and how it specifically impacts anxiety. In a 2010 study conducted by Amanda Mercer MS, LGPC, and colleagues at Eastern Virginia Medical School, it was shown that visual journaling created a general decrease in anxiety and negative affect levels—the amount of distress, anxiety, and dissatisfaction expressed and experienced—among the test population.

Similarly, a 2018 study conducted for the *Journal of Medical Internet Research* found that less than ten minutes of positive affect journaling each day decreased participants' depression and anxiety symptoms while increasing their overall resilience after just one month. Positive affect journaling is defined as an emotion-focused and self-regulation writing intervention.

Overall, the evidence supports the idea that regular journal practice is something that can greatly benefit those with anxiety and can be a useful tool for reducing anxious thoughts and ruminating. Journaling really is a simple but powerful micro-habit to help combat and reduce your anxiety.

How to Journal

Like meditating, the first step in starting a journaling practice is just to do it. Start somewhere! Put pen to paper. Any written record of thoughts, feelings, and experiences is journaling. The biggest hurdle is to sit down and let it happen.

Over the next eight weeks, this journal will help you cultivate a daily practice. You will find a large array of journaling practices in these pages, from freewriting to visual (drawing) journaling, letter writing to list-making. Do your best to leave judgment at the door, release any desire you have to censor or edit what you write down, and let the words flow. Some days the words may come easily, and other days there may be resistance. That's okay! Just keep going, do your best, know that the benefits are happening, and trust the process.

I know you can do this!

week 1

ACKNOWLEDGING & ACCEPTING THE PRESENCE OF ANXIETY

Every journey starts with a single step.

The first step of this journey is acknowledging and accepting that anxiety is a part of life. Anxiety can take many forms. It can manifest in unique ways for different people. So, looking your anxiety square in the eye and getting a clear picture of what you are dealing with is the best place to start.

This week, you will build a strong foundation in meditation and journaling. You will peel back the curtain to discover where your anxiety is showing up in your life and take your first steps toward acknowledging and accepting the role it plays in your daily routines. You will examine how anxiety manifests in your day-to-day life and what it feels like, and try to identify the origins of your anxious thoughts.

We know that anxiety stems from the fight or flight instinct, which, at its core, is a survival mechanism. While this instinct can be useful during times of survival and great stress, we don't need to experience it all the time. Learning how to distinguish between the anxiety that keeps us alive and the anxiety that keeps us from living can be the first step in releasing the hold it has on our sympathetic nervous system. This will ultimately help us lead a more balanced, less fraught life.

Before you start working on detaching yourself from anxious thoughts, you need to first take inventory of them and recognize what is happening within and around you. So, welcome to the first step of this journey. Each day will bring you closer to realizing that you are not your thoughts.

For this week, set a timer for 8 minutes for each daily meditation practice. Remember, the first step is always the hardest, so even this small commitment is huge. I hope you honor and celebrate yourself for showing up.

Daily Mantra

In moments of anxiety, I welcome calm.

Daily Practice

Close your eyes and begin to inhale for a count of 4 and exhale for a count of 7. Do this 10 times. Then, visualize yourself sitting at a café with your anxiety and coexisting. Get a clear picture of who your anxiety is, what it looks like, and how it's showing up in your life. When your time is complete, take a deep breath in through the nose and out through the mouth to close your practice.

Write about what you saw during your meditation. Who is your anxiety? What does it look like? How is it showing up in your life right now?

Daily Mantra

Each moment is temporary, and this will soon be in the past.

Guided Practice

Visualize yourself sitting on a beach, near the ocean's shore. See yourself quietly sitting, watching, and listening as the waves cascade up and down the shoreline. Allow yourself to sit with the ocean's waves. They come, they go, you watch them, but they don't affect you. Your anxiety is like the water. It can't always be controlled, but you can accept its existence, sit with it, and learn how to live with it without it affecting you.

Below is space for two numbered lists. In the first list, write 5 things that you can control today. In the second list, write 5 things that are out of your control.

IN MY CONTROL

OUT OF MY CONTROL

1

1

2

2

3

3

4

4

5

5

Daily Mantra

I am more than my anxiety.

Guided Practice

Get a small mirror or go into a room with a mirror. Close your eyes and take 3 deep breaths. Then, open your eyes and gaze into the mirror without judgment. Look past your eyes and into your deepest self. Connect with the person that is beyond your anxiety. How does this person act, how do they feel? Who are they? Take time to connect with them as you continue to reflect and gaze until your time is up.

Write down what words came up during your meditation practice. How do you perceive yourself today? Without judgment, write the words that came to mind. Who are you without your anxiety?

Daily Mantra

I take life one moment at a time.

Guided Practice

Begin the practice by connecting to your breath. Follow the pathway the air takes as it moves in and out of your nose. On the inhale, feel the air move into the nose, across the sinuses, and down the throat to the expanding lungs. Then, feel this process reverse itself naturally on the exhale. Stay present with the breath as it travels in and out of your body, as you practice "noting" in your journal.

As anxious or random thoughts pop up during your meditation, write them down in the space below. For example, if you think *I need to go to the store today* write down "grocery store." Or if you worry about turning off the oven, write down "oven." Then, when you're done, look for common themes in your notes.

Daily Mantra

Today I honor my needs.

Guided Practice

Bring your awareness into your space and into the moment. Take a few minutes to check in with your body, mind, and heart today. First, ask yourself, *How does my body feel today?* Then, *What thoughts am I having today?* Then, *What feelings am I experiencing today?* Finally, based on all this input, *How am I really doing today?*

Write down a recipe for your perfect day: ingredients and instructions. What would be a part of that day? What would your routine look like? After you've created your recipe, circle one ingredient or instruction that you can and will do today.

Daily Mantra

Safety and security surround me.

Guided Practice

Visualize a sparkling, iridescent bubble. Watch as this bubble grows and surrounds you, forming a protective barrier between you and the world. All your anxious thoughts, symptoms, and experiences are being pulled outside of the bubble, and inside, you are left free from the burden of your anxiety. Look at what is outside of that bubble and what is inside. Continue to breathe and with each breath, imagine the bubble growing bigger and stronger, keeping you safe and calm, moving your anxiety further away from you.

Draw your bubble and write down what you saw outside of it and inside of it.

Daily Mantra

My anxiety does not define me.

Guided Practice

Imagine a day without anxiety. What would it feel like? What would you do differently? Imagine an entire day in detail from beginning to end completely free from anxiety.

Draw a cross on the page, separating the page into 4 quadrants. Label one of each quadrant body, mind, heart, and relationships. In each of the 4 sections, fill out how your anxiety is showing up in in these categories.

week 2
ANXIETY IN THE BODY

*The body may only feel a sensation for a moment,
but it can remember it for a lifetime.*

The first place we notice anxiety is often in our bodies. The sweaty palms, the tight chest, the rapid heartbeat. The physical feelings of anxiety can be intense, immediate, and all-consuming. At times, it can feel like we're on a roller coaster moving a million miles an hour without a way to stop, just going up and down.

As we know, the body is designed to react, adapt, remember, and survive. In these moments of intense physical anxiety, it is important to remember that what you're experiencing is nothing more than a physiological response to a stressor or trigger. All that's needed to achieve quick and immediate relief, and finally get off the roller coaster, are a few simple go-to tools for soothing the nervous system, calming the body, and quieting the nerves.

This week, you will focus on creating those tools and adding them to your toolbox, learning quick but powerful techniques and practices to use whenever you feel the physical sensations of anxiety beginning. Then, once you have identified your unique symptoms, you can dial into what you need, learn how your body responds, develop your formula for achieving physical relief, and learn more about how your body reacts and adapts to anxiety.

Learning how to soften anxiety spikes by dialing in to the body is a foundational part of the practice you're developing with this journal, but as you dive in, don't forget to be kind to yourself, approach it with an open mind, and remember that the body can surprise you. The anxiety you are physically feeling is a switch being turned on, and if you turn it on, you can absolutely turn it off.

This week, set your timer for 9 minutes for your daily meditation practice. Good luck!

Daily Mantra

Each inhale brings me peace. Each exhale allows me to release.

Guided Practice

Take a few big, deep breaths to settle in. Return your breath to normal, but let it slow down while you tune in to your body. Feel where your body is connecting to the floor or surface beneath you. Imagine the ground is a magnet that gently draws out all anxiety and worry from the physical body where it is absorbed and recycled by the Earth. Then, imagine that through the crown of your head, you are drawing calm into your body. With each inhale, draw calm into the body from the crown. With each exhale, release anxiety and worry from your physical body into the Earth. Continue this circuit of breathing and releasing until your body feels calm and relaxed.

Below is space for two numbered lists. In the first list, write 5 things you are ready to release today. In the second, list 5 things you are ready to welcome into your body to help you find calm.

READY TO RELEASE   READY TO WELCOME IN

1   1

2   2

3   3

4   4

5   5

Daily Mantra

I quiet my mind and soften my body.

Guided Practice

Begin by taking a few moments to connect with your breath. Breathe consciously, slowing down your breath to a calm, even pace. Then, bring your awareness to the tips of your toes. Begin a body scan at your toes and slowly move your attention up your body: ankles, legs, hips, etc. At each part, pause to check in with how it's feeling. Is there any anxiety stored there? Send one breath to each part of your body before moving on, until you have scanned through your entire body, ending with the top of the head.

Where in your body do you feel your anxiety the most? What does it feel like physically? What sensations are you experiencing? Brainstorm ideas for what you can do for that part of your body to help release the anxiety, worry, and stress that is appearing there. For example, going for a walk outside will help you release your anxiety into the Earth or doing a yoga flow will help you release the tension from your muscles.

Daily Mantra

My breath brings me peace.

Guided Practice

First, get in a comfortable position where you can breathe effortlessly. Then, bring your awareness to your breath. Follow it in and out of your body as you inhale and exhale. Take a mental scan of your body, checking in with how it is feeling. Then, begin to practice feather breathing: Inhale fully through your nose and then exhale through slightly pursed lips, as if you're blowing a feather from your lips up into the air. Continue breathing like this, visualizing the body slowing down and becoming calmer with each exhale.

MINDFUL IN MINUTES: YOU ARE NOT YOUR THOUGHTS

Jot down a list of 10 things that you find calming. Once you have your list, pick 3 of them and brainstorm ways you can incorporate those things into your everyday life during moments of anxiety.

1	6
2	7
3	8
4	9
5	10

Daily Mantra

I find gratitude in the small moments.

Guided Practice

Begin your practice by taking 3 deep breaths, feeling the chaos of life begin to slow down with each breath out. Now place your palms together in front of you in a prayer position and rub them together quickly and firmly until they feel warm. Place your warm hands on a part of your body where you feel tension or stress. Let the warmth of your hands absorb into that part of your body, diffusing the stress and tension. Repeat this practice until you have warmed and released all the tense areas on your body.

Write down 8 things, big or small, that are going well in your life right now.

1

2

3

4

5

6

7

8

Daily Mantra

I give my body what it needs daily.

Guided Practice

Today, you are going to spend 10 minutes engaging in mindful movement. This could be gentle yoga, going for a walk, stretching, dancing, or anything that feels good for your body. Don't overthink it, but do be fully present with your body as you move it in a nourishing way. Ready? Set your timer for 10 minutes and go!

Write down 5 simple ways you can honor and nourish your body through movement today.

1

2

3

4

5

Daily Mantra

There is no danger. I am safe in this moment.

Guided Practice

Today, you'll practice a progressive relaxation technique called "tense and release." This technique involves cycling through parts of the body, intentionally clenching your muscles to create tension during your inhale, then completely releasing the muscles, letting go of all tension, on the exhale. First, bring your attention to your body. Start with your feet, clenching them on the inhale and releasing them fully on the exhale. Then move up to your legs, then hips, abdomen, etc., until you've completely tensed and released every major muscle group in your body. Then, do one final full body tense and release, coming into a full state of body relaxation afterward. End your meditation by taking a few deep breaths into your relaxed body.

Where in your body do you experience the most physical anxiety? Reflect on the places you felt the most sensation during the tense and release practice. Then, write down one thing you can do to soften those areas quickly when you feel tension starting to creep in. For example, if you get tension in your chest, perhaps you reach your hands behind your back for a chest expansion to open the muscles between the ribs.

Daily Mantra

*I release the past, I respect the future,
and I live in the now.*

Guided Practice

Start your practice by taking a few deep breaths to clear your mind. Close your eyes and picture yourself standing in a lush, green, safe, and friendly forest. Open all your senses to the scenery around you. Notice what you see, smell, feel, and hear in this forest. The energy is calming and grounding. Visualize yourself going on a walk in the forest, absorbing the calm energy and keeping your senses open to whatever appears.

Write about a place where you feel the most at ease. Is it in this forest? Your favorite vacation spot? Your home? Describe how you feel there and what makes it feel calm and safe.

week 3
ANXIETY IN THE MIND

Thoughts are like drops of water. They seem small and insignificant until you see the ripples that reach far beyond the initial drop.

Before you can separate yourself from your thoughts and release the grip they have on your life, you need to be able to see them clearly and understand where they're coming from.

Anxious thoughts tend to live in the shadows, affecting us even when we're not consciously aware they exist. To recognize anxious thoughts and see how they're manifesting in your life, you have to shine a light on the shadows of your mind, illuminating what is hiding in the darkness. Once you've brought these negative thoughts out into the light, it becomes much easier to release them.

Think of this week as if you were taking inventory before a big organizational project. Before you can release anything and bring order to the clutter, you must first pull everything out and see what you have. Decide what is worth keeping and what is not, and then organize it accordingly.

This week, you will look into all the nooks and crannies of your mind and get a clear picture of exactly what thoughts you're holding onto, so when the time comes to release them, you will be able to do so with clarity and ease.

As you work through this week, keep reminding yourself that you and your thoughts are separate things. You are safe. Your thoughts do not have control over you. All you're doing is taking inventory of what you're holding onto mentally. As you shine a light into your mind, rely on what you learned in weeks one and two to keep yourself from getting overwhelmed. Acknowledge your thoughts, but avoid clutching onto them, and utilize the practices from week two to soothe your body if you feel the physical sensations of anxiety reappear.

This week, set your timer for 10 minutes for each daily meditation practice.

Daily Mantra

Inhale calm, exhale anxiety.

Guided Practice

Today, you'll practice a relaxation breath to help soothe your nervous system and quiet your mind. Close your eyes and get comfortable. Begin to breathe deeply into your belly until you find an effortless breath pattern. After a few moments, begin your relaxation breath by inhaling for a count of 4 and exhaling for a count of 7. Imagine anxiety and worry leaving your body on every exhale, and peace and calm entering your body on every inhale. Continue to do this for the remainder of your time.

What thoughts kept coming into your mind when you were meditating? What is the likelihood of these thoughts coming true? Rank them from 1 to 5 on the likelihood of coming true (1 not likely, 5 very likely).

Daily Mantra

My mind is still, and my thoughts are clear.

Guided Practice

Settle into your practice by taking 3 deep breaths. Then, imagine that you are holding a clear crystal ball. As you breathe into your belly, watch your anxiety being pulled from your body and mind and absorbed into the crystal. As you release more of your anxious thoughts and feelings, see the crystal begin to change from clear to dark grey. When your 10 minutes are up, close your practice by visualizing the crystal being buried deep in the earth, separating you from your anxiety forever.

Draw a picture of what was in your crystal ball during your meditation,
labeling the thoughts and feelings that you drew.

Daily Mantra

My thoughts do not define me.

Guided Practice

Today, we'll explore a practice called "alternate nostril breathing." Begin with 3 deep breaths. Then, hold your left nostril closed with your right ring finger and inhale through the right nostril. At the top of your inhale, press the right nostril closed with your thumb, release your ring finger, and exhale through the left nostril. Keep your fingers as they are and inhale again through the left nostril. Plug the left with your ring finger, release the thumb, and exhale through the right. This is one round. Continue with this breath for 15 rounds, imagining that every time the breath passes across your sinuses, it erases anxious thoughts from your mind. With any remaining time, release your hands and practice a simple, effortless breath out of both nostrils equally.

What time of day do you find you have the most anxious thoughts? Does anything specific seem to trigger them?

Daily Mantra

During moments of anxiety, I find calm within.

Guided Practice

Today, you'll focus on your senses to pull yourself out of anxious thought patterns and back into the present moment. Begin by taking a few moments to drop into your body and center yourself. Then, take 3 deep breaths. Now, key into your surroundings. Looking around your space, name 5 things you see, then 5 things you feel, then 5 things you hear. Repeat this 3 times, finding new things to focus on with each cycle. With any remaining time, practice a balancing breath, in which your inhales and exhales are even in length. A count of 4 is a good length for this practice.

Write a list of 5 anxious thoughts you have frequently. Then rewrite them in a positive and truthful way. For example, "Bad things happen when it is raining" could turn into "My day is not impacted by the weather."

ANXIOUS THOUGHTS   POSITIVE TRUTHS

1   1

2   2

3   3

4   4

5   5

Daily Mantra

I see the thought and look for the truth.

Guided Practice

Begin by bringing your awareness to the tip of your nose. Start to slow down your breath, making it intentional and deep. Notice the cool air as it moves into your body at the tip of your nose on the inhale, and then experience the warm air leaving your body at the tip of the nose as you exhale. Do this for 10 rounds. Then, as you continue to breathe, on the inhale think *I welcome truth into my mind* and on the exhale think *Anxiety leaves with my breath*. Continue to breathe and repeat this mantra as you focus on the tip of your nose.

Below are four boxes labeled "Thought," "Feeling," "Belief," and "Truth." Fill out the boxes by writing down an anxious thought in the first box, how it makes you feel in the second, the belief that forms the base of that thought in the third, and the truth about this thought in the final box. For example, the thought might be *Everyone is looking at me and thinks I'm weird*, the feeling might be *Self-conscious, nervous, isolated*, the belief may be something like *I am unlikeable*, but the truth is *Most people aren't looking at me or worried about what I'm doing*. Fill the boxes with as many thoughts and truths as you need.

THOUGHT

FEELING

BELIEF

TRUTH

Daily Mantra

*I find ease and clarity in moments
of anxiety.*

Guided Practice

Come to a comfortable position and take 3 or more
deep breaths to clear your mind. When you feel
settled, visualize a stream of running water in front of
you. As you breathe, watch the water flow toward you,
past you, and away from you. When intrusive thoughts
pop into your mind, visualize them as tiny leaves that
drop into the stream of your thoughts. The leaves float
on the water, moving down the stream. You notice
them as they drift past, but they don't bother you, and
eventually, they're swept away by the current.

Draw the stream in the space below (grab crayons or colored pencils if you'd like). Allow yourself to draw without judgment, filling the stream with small leaves that are floating, just like your anxious thoughts. Let your creativity come out to play today.

Daily Mantra

I exist independently of my anxious thoughts.

Guided Practice

Begin by taking a few deep breaths, and repeating today's mantra, *I exist independently of my anxious thoughts*, 5 times in your mind, or aloud. Take a mental scan of your body and notice any places where you're squeezing or clenching. Soften these places. Next, visualize yourself sitting in your meditation position holding a balloon. As anxious thoughts appear in your mind, take them out of your head and place them in the balloon. Over time, the balloon gets fuller and fuller as your mind becomes clear of these thoughts. Close your practice by releasing the balloon and letting it float away into the sky.

Draw a big balloon on your page. In that balloon, write down every anxious thought you're currently having or have had recently until it's filled up. When you are done, imagine yourself releasing the balloon or popping it, letting go of all that was in it.

week 4
ANXIETY IN THE HEART

Feelings are something that you experience;
they are not who you are.

We all know what anxiety feels like in our heart. The nervousness, the worry, the ache in our core that ripples out into our lives, coloring our daily experiences and our relationships. It's easy to allow anxiety to hijack your emotions and send you into a spiral, so this week you will focus on hitting the pause button and releasing the grip anxiety has on your feelings and emotions.

Anxiety is a very emotional experience but remember, like the physical sensations that you explored in week two, the feelings you're experiencing here are a byproduct of a neurological switch being turned on in response to a stressor. If that switch can turn on, it can also turn off. This week, you will learn how to cope with those feelings in the same way you coped with your physical symptoms and anxious thoughts in weeks two and three.

For week four, you will connect to your heart center, exploring your emotional reactions to anxiety triggers, and finding ways to bring relief to your heart. Meditation and journaling are great tools for emotional exploration but sometimes initially can result in discomfort, particularly if you are someone who avoids connecting with your feelings.

As you journey into the heart space this week, remember to tread softly and with compassion. Try your best to avoid labeling your feelings as "good" or "bad." Instead, think of each emotion that arises as giving you information, telling you what you're experiencing and what you need. All feelings are valid and significant, even unpleasant ones. Most importantly, remember that you are worthy and deserving of relief from your anxiety and the pain it causes in your heart.

For this week, set your timer for 11 minutes for each daily meditation practice.

Daily Mantra

I am safe, I am loved, I am present in the now.

Guided Practice

For the first few minutes of your session, settle into your practice by following your breath in and out of your body through your nose. When you feel settled in and fully connected to your breath, add a loving kindness mantra to your practice, repeating it with each breath. A few options are:

I am safe.

I am loved.

My breath brings me peace.

I am safe, I am loved, I am present in the now.

Repeat these for at least 5 minutes. Close your practice by sending love and kindness to yourself.

Think of one person you can always rely on in your life. What do they do to make you feel loved and safe? How can you recreate these feelings for yourself?

Daily Mantra

Each moment is temporary, and this will soon be in the past.

Guided Practice

Begin today's practice by slowing down your breath and sending it low into your belly. When you're ready, visualize a pink light surrounding your heart. The light is bright and warm, and it melts away anxiety, worry, and stress. The deeper you breathe, the stronger the pink light becomes, melting away all the anxious and worrisome feelings. Continue to breathe, visualize the light, and let it melt the unwanted feelings from your heart center until the meditation comes to an end.

Below is space for two numbered lists. In the first, list 5 things that you choose to release from your heart today. In the second, list 5 things you will welcome into your heart.

RELEASING

WELCOMING IN

1

1

2

2

3

3

4

4

5

5

Daily Mantra

*I honor how I feel and welcome compassion
into my heart.*

Guided Practice

Today you will practice a self-compassion meditation. Begin by getting comfortable and placing your hands over your heart, allowing your chest to absorb the heat from your hands. Sit, breathe, and hold space for the emotions you're experiencing today, naming them as they arise. Then, visualize a warm, compassionate wave of energy coming out of your hands and surrounding your heart. This wave sends compassion to yourself for the emotions you are experiencing. Focus on that feeling and close the meditation by hugging yourself and telling yourself something kind.

With the feeling of self-compassion still resonating in your heart, write a letter to yourself that you can read when you're struggling and in need of comfort or healing from your anxiety. Tell yourself whatever you would need to hear in those moments and save it to reread when you need it.

Daily Mantra

My body tells me what I need to know.

Guided Practice

This meditation revolves around a body scan. Start at your feet and slowly move up toward your ankles, legs, and so on until you reach the top of your head. At each part of your body, check-in and notice if you are experiencing any physical sensations of an emotion there. For example, you may feel a physical sensation of sadness in your eyes in the form of pressure or held-back tears. When you come across a physical manifestation of feelings in your body, name the emotion. Take time to be with your feelings by taking a few deep breaths and experiencing the emotions and sensations that arise.

Draw a full-body picture (even a stick figure!) of yourself. Circle the parts of the body in which you physically experience emotion. Identify which emotions they are and what they feel like.

Daily Mantra

I allow my emotions to flow freely from my heart.

Guided Practice

Begin your practice by slowing down your breath and sending it down low into your belly. Focus your attention on your heart and connect to whatever sensations are occurring there. There may be a lot that begins to well up—that's okay! Visualize your heart center opening and allowing whatever is built up to pour out of you like a waterfall. See your feelings pouring from your heart out onto the ground until you feel you have released everything that was stored there.

Draw a waterfall and write down the feelings that came pouring from your heart in your meditation, taking time to honor each one as you write it.

Daily Mantra

My heart is filled with love and light.

Guided Practice

Begin your practice with a relaxed breath. Inhale for a count of 4 and exhale for a count of 6. Do this until you feel your body begin to physically soften and relax. Then, release the count and feel your breath flowing effortlessly, low, and slowly into the belly. In your mind's eye, visualize yourself laying on a beach under the sun. Listen to the waves, smell the salt, and enjoy the warmth of the sun shining down on your heart center, melting away all sadness, anxiety, or unwanted emotions from your heart.

Write down 6 ways that you can soothe yourself emotionally when you experience moments of heaviness or discomfort in the heart. Brainstorm things that instantly bring your heart happiness and light.

1

2

3

4

5

6

Daily Mantra

I honor who I am past, present, and future.

Guided Practice

Recall a memory where you felt loved and appreciated unconditionally. Reflect on this feeling and draw it into your physical body. Let this feeling pour through you and move throughout your body until you feel full of love, kindness, and respect. Visualize your past self and send these feelings to them, without judgment. Do the same with your future self and, finally, your present self.

Below are three columns labeled "Past," "Present," and "Future." Write down 3 kind and respectful facts about yourself in each of these times in your life.

PAST   PRESENT   FUTURE

week 5
SOOTHING YOUR ANXIETY

A soothing sanctuary exists within you that you can retreat to any time you need.

Congratulations! You're halfway through this journal. This deserves a moment of celebration! Honor the work you've done so far and give yourself a little high-five or hug, because you've come a long way!

For the last four weeks, you've focused on accepting and acknowledging your anxiety, and recognizing how it shows up in your body, mind, and heart while gathering tools for your anxiety toolbox along the way. Each meditation and journal prompt has taught you more about your anxiety and has given you a technique to help you work through and soothe your anxious thoughts. This week, you are going to start putting those techniques to work.

As we dive into week five (and the second half of this journal), you'll start putting together the puzzle pieces you've been gathering to get a full picture of how you can soothe your anxiety in the moment and begin detaching yourself from it. The immediate goal of this week is to reduce the pain or discomfort of anxiety on the spot by using what you're learning in your practices. As you move through the week, I ask that you do so with compassion and curiosity as you begin to put your tools to work and use your practices to help you soothe yourself when anxiety strikes.

Each person will experience anxiety differently, and therefore some tools may work better for you than for others. This is about learning what works best for you. Now that you've begun to understand how your anxiety works, it's time to get to work creating your own soothing recipe for finding that safe sanctuary within.

For this week, set your meditation timer for 11 minutes.

Daily Mantra

*Experience gives me what I need
to take action.*

Guided Practice

Bring your awareness to the small space below
your nose and above your lip. Breathe naturally,
sending the breath down into your belly, and
focus on the temperature of the breath in this
small space as it moves in and out of your body.
Now, begin to count your breaths beginning
at one. Think inhale, 1; exhale, 2; and continue
to breathe and count until you reach 100. Then
begin counting back down from 100 to 1 until
the meditation ends.

Below are two circles you're going to use to make pie charts. The first circle represents where your anxiety manifests: body, mind, and heart. Divide that circle between those three places, assigning a percentage value to how often your anxiety shows up in each one. The second circle represents when your anxiety shows up: morning, afternoon, and night. Divide that circle between those three times, assigning a percentage to each one depending on how often you experience anxiety at that time. Take note of the top percentage for each pie chart. This will help you identify those times when you are most likely to need extra soothing and what tools to reach for to soothe it.

WHERE MY ANXIETY
OCCURS

WHEN MY ANXIETY
OCCURS

Daily Mantra

I trust the universe has a plan for me.

Guided Practice

Today you will practice the ancient meditation technique of candle gazing. Light a candle and look at the dancing flame with a gentle gaze. Let your eyes be soft as they rest on the light. If you're unable to light a candle in your space, visualize one in your mind and watch it slowly burn, flicker, and dance within your mind's eye. As you watch the candle, practice a balancing breath by inhaling for a count of 4 and exhaling for a count of 4.

Create a "soothing vision board" in the space below. Cut out and tape images from magazines, online printouts, etc., that bring you a feeling of calm and peace of mind. Do this in any way that feels intuitive—there is no right or wrong way—and allow yourself to look at them any time you need a soothing boost. You can also do a bigger version of this on a larger piece of paper or board outside this journal.

Daily Mantra

*I protect my peace; only good
comes into my space.*

Guided Practice

Begin by taking a few deep breaths. Check in with how
you're feeling and what thoughts you're having today.
Honor what you're experiencing, then give yourself
permission to set it aside for the next few minutes. Slow
down your breath and visualize a white protective bubble of light beginning to form around your body. With
each breath, this bubble grows bigger, stronger, and
brighter, creating a protective barrier around you. Once
your bubble is complete, enjoy your time sitting quietly
in your protective bubble that cannot be penetrated by
stress, anxiety, worry, or intrusive thoughts.

Write down 5 simple things you can do to protect your peace today.

1

2

3

4

5

Daily Mantra

Every part of me is worthy of peace and harmony.

Guided Practice

Visualize yourself laying on a blanket outside, under the stars. You feel safe and secure here. It's a beautiful summer night. Imagine the sounds of nighttime around you. As you lay under the stars and breathe, see the moon rising overhead. Watch the big, full, silvery moon rise. When it's finally overhead, feel its calming light shine down on your body, soothing any anxiety, stress, or worry you are feeling. This is a quiet, safe space for you to breathe and be still under the moonlight.

Listed below are eight topics that commonly cause people to experience anxiety: work, family, friends, romantic relationships, health, travel, finances, and community/ social interactions. Assign each category a number rating from 1 to 10 (1 being not very much, and 10 being a lot) based on how much it is contributing to your anxiety today. For anything rated higher than 7, write down one thing you can do today to lower that rating. If time permits, repeat the rating exercise tonight or tomorrow morning and see if the ratings have changed based on the actions you took to soothe your anxiety in each category.

CATEGORY	RATING	SOLUTION
Work		
Family		
Friends		
Romantic Relationships		
Health		
Travel		
Finances		
Community/ Social Interactions		

Daily Mantra

Inhale—my mind is clear.
Exhale—I release negative thoughts.

Guided Practice

Today you will practice a technique called "spinal breathing." Begin by closing your eyes and checking in with yourself. Then, bring your awareness to the base of the spine. Imagine the spine like a straw: As you inhale, the breath is drawn up from the base of the spine to the crown of the head; as you exhale, the breath falls back from the crown to the base of the spine. Watch and feel the breath dance up and down your spine with each inhale and exhale. If you want, assign the breath a soothing color and imagine light in that color moving up and down your spine with the breath.

Below is a drawing of a large, lidless jar. This is your "worry jar." Write down different anxious thoughts that you are ready to release in the jar. Fill the jar up with these thoughts. When you are done, repeat to yourself *I am not my thoughts* 3 times and draw a lid on the jar. Then, close your journal, leaving these thoughts in the jar forever.

Daily Mantra
I find happiness in the present moment.

Guided Practice

Today's practice is a walking meditation. Set your timer and step outside for a slow, intentional walk using all your senses. Try to avoid distractions like music or texts during this session. Instead, focus on what is happening within you and around you as you stay present with each step you take and allow each one to be slow and intentional.

If you aren't able to go outside, do this meditation as a visualization. Picture yourself going on a walk in your preferred area, focusing on what you see, hear, smell, and feel along the way.

What distracted you the most during your walk? What did you find the most pleasant? How can you incorporate these elements into your everyday life?

Daily Mantra

Peace surrounds me.

Guided Practice

You'll be working with color today. Choose a color that you feel represents calm and inner peace and a color that represents anxiety. Hold these colors in your mind. Begin to focus on your breath, feeling it move in and out of your body. Slow down your breath, send it deep into your belly, and begin expanding your exhales so they are a bit longer than your inhales. Then, as you inhale, imagine breathing the calming color into your body, filling up all your cells one at a time. As you exhale, imagine yourself releasing the color representing anxiety, letting it pour out of you in a stream of breath. Continue breathing this way until you feel your body has released all the negative color and is filled only with the calm color.

When you are feeling triggered, what are three simple forms of self-care (aside from meditation and journaling) that you can practice to soothe your anxiety responses?

1

2

3

week 6
REFRAMING YOUR ANXIETY

Change the way you look at things, and things start changing the way they look.

Welcome to week six! This week, you will be striving to look at your anxiety in a new way and reframe how you think about it. Reframing isn't about pretending something is good or true when it isn't, but about discovering what could be good and true about that thing if you changed the way you look at it. To reframe your anxiety is to look at it with a new perspective and potentially create a new outcome for your experience with it.

Reframing your relationship with anxiety—particularly recognizing that it is something that happens to you, not something that *is* you—is an essential step in learning to detach yourself from your thoughts. You and your anxiety are separate entities, coexisting in life. They are not the same, and if you change the way you look at and think about your anxiety, suddenly it starts to change the way it looks (for the better!).

Like an iceberg, anxiety often presents itself as something different above the surface than below. We tend to focus on what we see on the surface, but when we dive beneath the water and look at what is underneath, it gives us a new perspective, helping us to reframe our understanding of the experience and better understand where it's coming from. Suddenly, you have a different picture in your mind about what your anxiety is and what it can be. Suddenly, you are able to find new connections and patterns in your anxiety that make it easier to move beyond and let go.

This week, you will explore seven meditation and journaling exercises that will change the way you see your anxiety and ask you to reframe how you think about it on a day-to-day basis.

Set your meditation timer for 11 minutes this week.

Daily Mantra

I have the power to reframe my thoughts.

Guided Practice

Visualize yourself sitting in a quiet and comforting place with your favorite cup of coffee or tea. Feel the warmth of the cup in your hands and smell its aroma. As you breathe, imagine yourself slowly taking small sips of this drink. With each sip, feel the warmth begin to spread further through your body, magically transforming unpleasant feelings into the pleasant opposites of those feelings.

In this prompt, you'll practice reframing unpleasant feelings. Below are two columns labeled "Unpleasant Emotions" and "Reframing." In the first column, write down an unpleasant emotion you frequently experience, such as "isolation" or "insecurity." In the next column, try to reframe that emotion or experience in a more positive way. For example, "isolation" might be reframed as "living independently." "Insecurity" might be reframed as "heightened awareness of self." Fill the columns with as many emotions and reframing as you need.

UNPLEASANT EMOTIONS   REFRAMING

Daily Mantra

I trust my inner guide.

Guided Practice

Begin your meditation with 3 deep, cleansing breaths. Visualize yourself sitting in meditation and make note of where you are experiencing any symptoms of anxiety in your body, heart, and mind. Now turn inward, looking past those symptoms, and see if you can connect with the core or center of your experience. Ask yourself, *What is at the center of my anxiety?* and see if an answer appears. Be patient, listen, and just see what happens. If you don't hear anything—that's okay!

In the space below, draw an iceberg that represents how you experience anxiety. Fill the top of the iceberg with the symptoms and sensations of anxiety you experience every day. In the bottom of the iceberg, beneath the water, write down what you think the root cause of those daily symptoms might be.

Daily Mantra

I take life one day at a time.

Guided Practice

Begin your meditation by doing some small, intuitive movements to connect to your body, such as a few yoga poses or gentle stretches. Once connected to your body, begin to breathe deeply, and visualize a white orb that looks like a small moon hovering over the top of your head. On your next exhale, see that moon orbit down the backside of your body, landing at the base of your spine. On your inhale, visualize the moon orbiting up the front of your body, landing back at the crown of your head, completing a full circle around your seated figure. Continue this orbital breath with each inhale and exhale, watching the moon orbit up and down the front and back of your body.

Think about what cycles you may find yourself engaging in daily that are not contributing to your well-being. For example, you may find that you wake up and immediately check social media on your phone, which prompts a feeling of lack or insufficiency, which then kicks off your anxiety symptoms. Write down any similar cycles in your life that are not serving your highest good and inner peace and consider what you can do to start breaking those cycles today.

Daily Mantra

Inhale—courage. Exhale—fear.

Guided Practice

Begin your practice by giving yourself permission to honor how you're feeling today and how you're showing up in this moment. Then, visualize a yellow ball of light in the trunk of your body. This light is comforting, courageous, and brave. With each breath you take, the light grows bigger and brighter, filling you with the ability to face and work through fearful thoughts and physical anxiety. Keep breathing, allowing every cell in your body to absorb this energy until your whole body is filled top to toe with golden light and the courage to face your fears.

There are two types of fear: The fear that keeps you alive and the fear that keeps you from living. A fear of swimming with sharks keeps you alive, but a fear of what others think about you keeps you from living. Write a list of common fearful thoughts you have. After you have written this, circle all the fears that fall under the second category—the ones that keep you from living. Choose one and try to do something small today to conquer that fear.

Daily Mantra

I live independently of my anxious thoughts.

Guided Practice

Visualize yourself sitting by a window in a cozy cabin. Gaze outside and note your surroundings, taking in the beautiful view and wildlife. The sky is overcast, and it looks like rain. When an anxious thought comes up during your meditation, let that thought be a raindrop that hits the window of the cabin. Let the raindrops trickle down the window and disappear beneath the frame. Try not to attach yourself to these thoughts. Keep enjoying the view from your window and let the rain just be the weather.

Consider the anxious thoughts that came up during your meditation. For each thought, draw an individual raindrop and label it with that thought. Then, once you have written down all your thoughts, begin to label each raindrop as "helpful" or "true." If the thought is neither helpful nor true, put a line through it. When you're done, look at how many of those thoughts were helpful and/or true.

Daily Mantra

In moments of anxiety, I seek refuge in gratitude.

Guided Practice

As you settle in for your practice, give yourself permission to let go of whatever happened earlier today and whatever is happening later today, and just honor the present moment. Then, ignite a feeling of gratitude within you. Maybe you see gratitude as a color, or maybe it has a certain texture. Visualize gratitude surrounding you. Then begin radiating gratitude to individuals that love and support. End your practice by radiating gratitude to yourself.

In the space below, write down your typical routine for a normal day in your life. Be honest and detailed here; make sure you write down your actual routine, not your ideal one. When you've completed your list, go through your routine, and write "helps" next to the parts of your routine that help your feelings of anxiety and "hurts" next to the parts of your routine that contribute to your anxiety. Once you've labeled these, pick one of the "hurts" parts of your routine and write down an alternative that would turn this "hurt" into a "help." Repeat with the rest of the "hurts" until you have a full daily routine of "helps." Aim to make one of these swaps today.

Daily Mantra

I am rooted in the present moment.

Guided Practice

Come to a comfortable position and connect with your breath. Visualize yourself sitting in your space, breathing, and meditating. As you breathe, imagine roots growing down from your body, spreading wide and deep through the floor and into the earth. With each breath, see these roots grow deeper and stronger. Feel yourself bringing comfort, calm, and steadiness up through those roots with each inhale, and releasing all anxiety, worry, and stress through the roots on each exhale.

Consider all the work you've done in the last week. Based on all the practices and prompts, describe your current anxiety triggers and what you feel is at the root of them. Finish the entry by brainstorming ideas for what you can do or what you can tell yourself when you're feeling triggered to reframe the experience.

week 7
LIVING THROUGH ANXIETY

No matter how tall the mountain is, you can make the climb.

Remember the first week of this journal, when we talked about taking that first step? Well, I hope you're feeling proud of yourself—you took that step and look how far you've come since! At this point, hopefully you've hit your stride and are starting to notice changes in your life. Your daily meditation and journal practice should be feeling like a natural part of your routine at this point. Now, you just need to keep putting one foot in front of the other and keep making the climb.

This week, you will explore living through anxiety. You will use all the tools in your toolbox and practice living through and getting past moments of anxiety without getting swept away and paralyzed in your triggered moments. You will move your body, clear your mind, honor and soothe your feelings, and return again and again to the idea that anxiety is something that *happens* to you, not something that *is* you.

Anxiety may be something that ebbs and flows throughout your life. Though one day you hopefully will be completely free from its debilitating influence, chances are that instead of finding total freedom, you will instead learn how to manage your anxiety and coexist with this part of you—even if this part becomes much smaller over time. Think of this week as taking the training wheels off. You have the tools and skills to manage this part of your life and can now test them out in the real world, learning as you go. When anxiety rears its head, you know what to do.

This week, set your timer for 12 minutes of daily meditation, and remember it's called a *practice*, not a *perfect*. You are just exploring, trying your best, and making adjustments along the way. You've got this!

Daily Mantra

Anxiety is what I experience, it is not who I am.

Guided Practice

Make small movements to release any tension or restlessness in your body, like finding a chest expansion or dancing to your favorite song. Then, invite yourself to begin practicing stillness. First, allow yourself to become still physically, welcoming this sensation into your body. Then, welcome stillness into your thoughts, feeling its gentle coolness seep into your mind. Finally, welcome stillness into your heart, feeling your emotions even out and level off. Once you've found stillness in your body, mind, and heart, visualize yourself sitting at the ocean's edge. Feel the waves over your feet as the water moves in and out from the shore. Allow yourself to be completely unattached and unbothered by the waves, holding gently to the sensation of stillness, even as they dance up and down your feet.

Below, draw a ladder with 7 rungs. At the top of the ladder, write down an anxiety trigger or thought you're ready to overcome and how you will feel when you've released it. Then, label each rung of the ladder with one step or thing you can do to overcome this certain anxiety.

Daily Mantra

Every day, my peace grows.

Guided Practice

Begin to breathe deeply, sending each inhale low into your belly and allowing each exhale to be full and rich. Visualize yourself taking a seed of peace and inner harmony and planting it in the ground. As you continue to breathe deeply, visualize this seed sprouting, growing, and maturing. With each breath, this plant grows and matures until it is a full, lush, and thriving plant that emanates peace and inner harmony. End your practice by placing your hands around this plant and absorbing its energy into your being, welcoming peace and harmony into your day.

What small seeds of harmony and daily peace can you plant today
to create a significant impact in your everyday life?

Daily Mantra

Inhale—energy enters. Exhale—calm surrounds.

Guided Practice

As you settle in, notice the points of contact between your body and the surface beneath you. Ground yourself through these points and get comfortable in the moment, checking in with all your senses. Then, begin a 3-part breath. Take a small inhale, filling your lungs up about a third of the way. Pause briefly, then immediately take another small inhale, filling up another third of the way. Take one final short pause, followed by one final inhale that fills you up completely. Then take one long breath out. Repeat this 15 times, imagining you are bringing short bursts of energy into your body with each inhale and surrounding yourself with calm on the exhale. When you have done 15 rounds, settle into an effortless, steady breath, repeating your daily mantra for the remaining time: *inhale—energy enters, exhale—calm surrounds.*

Below are three boxes labeled "Energy," "Calm," and "Ritual." In the first box, make a list of things that give you energy. In the second box, write down things that bring you calm. In the final box, write down 3 new daily rituals you could create to incorporate things from boxes one and two.

ENERGY

CALM

RITUAL

Daily Mantra

I handle uncertainty with ease.

Guided Practice

Bring your awareness to the tip of your nose. Focus on the breath moving in and out of your body at this spot. Above the crown of your head, visualize a gold light. As you breathe, the light shines down on you, spreading over and surrounding your whole body, creating a sense of peace and certainty within you, and removing all feelings of worry, doubt, or uncertainty. You know that no matter what happens around you, you can find stillness and certainty within.

Write down a small pep talk you can read to yourself when you are facing moments of uncertainty. Think about what you would like to hear during those tough moments to remind you of how capable you are of navigating challenging times.

Daily Mantra
I release my false beliefs and honor my truth.

Guided Practice

Take 3 deep, cleansing breaths, allowing each exhale to release you further into a state of relaxation. Visualize yourself standing at the entryway of a vast, beautiful library. Take a moment to get a clear picture of it: stacks of books, rows of shelves, light streaming through the windows. Above the entrance to the library is a sign reading "Hall of Truth." See yourself walking into the library and taking a book that sticks out to you. This is a "truth book" and all that's written in it are true and positive statements about yourself. Spend time reading the statements in this book, taking in their honest, validating affirmations. When you're ready, open your eyes.

Imagine this page is a page in the "truth book" that you accessed during your meditation. Write down 5 false beliefs that you hold. Next to each one, write down a positive statement that you know is true. For example, "I am unlovable" may turn into "I am worthy of love every day."

1   FALSE: TRUE:

2   FALSE: TRUE:

3   FALSE: TRUE:

4   FALSE: TRUE:

5   FALSE: TRUE:

Daily Mantra

In moments of fear, I create safety within.

Guided Practice

Come to a comfortable position and do a quick mental scan of your body, noticing any areas where you feel tightness or tension. As you take a few deep breaths, allow these areas to soften and settle into your body. Visualize your dream cabin. This is your emotional safe house. Get a clear picture in your mind of what your cabin looks like, how big it is, and how it's decorated. See yourself standing in this anxiety-free space and make a note of what you have in the house and what it represents in the real world. For example, a cozy blanket might mean comfort. Then look out the window and see everything you left outside that's not allowed in your house, noting what those things represent in the real world as well.

Below is space for two numbered lists. In the first, write a list of 7 things that you will allow in your house. Focus on positive things such as problem-solving, rest, etc. In the second, list 7 things you will no longer allow in your house: over-thinking, self-criticism, etc.

THINGS *I WILL* ALLOW IN MY HOUSE

THINGS *I WILL NOT* ALLOW IN MY HOUSE

THINGS *I WILL* ALLOW IN MY HOUSE	THINGS *I WILL NOT* ALLOW IN MY HOUSE
1	1
2	2
3	3
4	4
5	5
6	6
7	7

Daily Mantra

I focus on what I can control and release what I cannot.

Guided Practice

Settle into your meditation by repeating the daily mantra, *I focus on what I can control and release what I cannot*, 5 times. Then focus your awareness on the points of contact between you and the floor, honing in on the grounding, calm energy of the earth beneath you. Then, shift your awareness to the crown of your head, focus on the uplifting, creative, and ethereal energy from above. Finally, bring your awareness to the center of your being and sit in stillness. Return to the daily mantra and repeat it as you breathe with your remaining time.

Below is space for two numbered lists. In the first list, write down 5 ways that you used to respond to feeling out of control. In the second list, write down 5 ways that you respond now, using the tools you've been practicing as a way to get a different, more positive outcome.

HOW I USED TO RESPOND

1

2

3

4

5

HOW I RESPOND NOW

1

2

3

4

5

week 8
MOVING BEYOND ANXIETY

When one journey ends, another one begins. Just keep going.

Y ou've done it. You've arrived at the final week. You have done so much work, and this week is where it all comes together. You may be feeling quite differently now. Your brain is most likely changing on a physical level to respond to triggers with smaller physiological anxiety symptoms and you have many tools in your anxiety toolbox that you know how to utilize.

You have faced your anxiety head-on; examined how it shows up in your body, mind, and heart; and worked to soothe and reframe your anxiety and coexist with it. This week, you'll fully embrace the understanding that you are not our thoughts, and anxiety is something that *happens* to you, not something that *is* you.

Although you have come so far already, think of this week as those final miles in a marathon. You can basically see the finish line, and this is the last push. Before you embark on this week's exercises, take a moment to remind yourself why you started this journal seven weeks ago, and what your initial goals were. Enjoy celebrating your progress over the next seven days.

Remember that even though this is the last week of the journal, it doesn't have to be the last week that you practice meditation and journaling as a habit. You're in the flow now and I encourage you to continue your new daily self-care habit beyond the pages of this journal, as long as they continue to have a positive effect in your life.

For this final week, set your daily meditation timer for 12 minutes.

Daily Mantra

My life is free from anxiety.

Guided Practice

For today's session, you're going to do a visualization where you picture an entire day of your life without anxiety. Imagine your ideal day as a person living anxiety-free. What would be different? What would you be able to do? How would you feel living this way? Go through your day from morning to night and watch it play out in front of you as you breathe and visualize this freedom from anxiety. End your meditation practice by welcoming this ideal day into your life. Allow yourself to go live this life today.

Think about the anxiety-free day you just imagined in your meditation. Write down the 5 biggest differences between that life and the one you're living now. Then, write down 5 actions you can take to make today more like that ideal day.

DIFFERENCES

ACTIONS

1

1

2

2

3

3

4

4

5

5

Daily Mantra

Things always work out for me.

Guided Practice

Visualize yourself laying in a hammock. You're in your favorite place, it's the perfect day, and your body is completely supported by the hammock as you gently sway side to side in the breeze. With each sway of the hammock, allow yourself to become more relaxed. Feel your mind become quieter and more peaceful as you breathe. As you meditate, just relax, enjoy the hammock, and know that all will be well.

Below are three boxes labeled "Week 1," "Week 8," and "Week 16." In the first box, write down how you were feeling in the first week of this journal. In the second box, write how these feelings have improved over the last eight weeks. In the third box, write down how you imagine yourself feeling in the next eight weeks, if you continue your daily practice.

WEEK 1

WEEK 8

WEEK 16

Daily Mantra

I am worthy and whole.

Guided Practice

Settle into your practice with some intuitive movement, such as finding a chest expansion, gentle yoga stretches, or anything that feels good to you. Close your eyes and turn your gaze inward, breathing deeply. Visualize yourself as a mosaic of distinct parts representing all the different facets of your personality. There's your anxious part, your confident part, your loving part, etc. Take time to imagine each of these pieces in detail: color, size, etc. Then, imagine them all coming together, one by one, to form a beautiful and whole you.

Using this week's meditation as inspiration, make an abstract drawing of all the different pieces of the personality mosaic you envisioned. Don't be afraid to get super creative here: Play with color, shape, size, and whatever else feels right. Label each piece and let them each be unique and representative of how that part of your personality feels to you.

Daily Mantra

Inhale—my body is safe.
Exhale—my mind is calm.

Guided Practice

If the weather permits, take your meditation outside today. Sit outside and open all your senses, focusing on what you hear, smell, taste, feel, and see, one at a time. Let nature be your point of concentration as you take in the moment of being outside and existing within a living, outdoor space. If you are unable to go outside, visualize yourself in your favorite place in nature and imagine what information you get from your senses.

Create a calm checklist for yourself that you can use every day. Write down seven small things that you can do each day to promote your well-being and mental health. Try to check them all off today!

YOUR CALM CHECKLIST

1 ☐

2 ☐

3 ☐

4 ☐

5 ☐

6 ☐

7 ☐

Daily Mantra

I have the power to release my anxiety.

Guided Practice

Place your hands in your lap, or anywhere that is comfortable, and turn your palms upward toward the sky (a gesture of opening and willingness). Repeat to yourself 3 times, *I am ready to release my anxiety and move forward with my life.* Like a magnet, watch your anxiety being pulled from your body, mind, and heart through your hands and out into the universe where it will be taken from you and turned into positive energy. Do this until you have felt a complete release.

Write down 3 things you are ready to leave behind you starting today, 3 things you are ready to start today, and 1 thing you currently do that you wish to continue.

LEAVE BEHIND TODAY

READY TO START TODAY

WISH TO CONTINUE

Daily Mantra

I am not my thoughts.

Guided Practice

Begin your meditation by taking 3 deep breaths, inhaling through your nose and exhaling it out through your mouth. Settle into a natural rhythm of breath that is low, slow, and effortless. Take a mental scan of your body, noticing anywhere you may still feel attached to your anxiety. This could manifest in many ways. There could be tightness or tension in the muscles, or a numbness in your hands and feet. Visualize this attachment as a golden thread that runs from you to your anxiety. Imagine a large pair of scissors cutting the thread and releasing the ties you have to your anxiety. With the remaining time, repeat the daily mantra as you breathe.

In today's meditation, you practiced cutting the tethers that tie you to your anxiety. Consider how you feel now that those tethers are cut. Below are three headers: "Body," "Mind," and "Heart." Under "Body," write how you feel different physically after the cord-cutting practice. Under "Mind," write how your thoughts have changed. And under "Heart," write how your feelings have changed now that these tethers have been released.

BODY

MIND

HEART

Daily Mantra

I celebrate my progress and honor my peace.

Guided Practice

Settle into your space by taking 3 deep, cleansing breaths. Follow your breath as it dances in and out of your body, focusing on the natural rise and fall of the belly as you breathe in and out. Now, begin a check-in with your body, mind, and heart, noticing what you are experiencing in each. After you have completed your check-in, return your focus to your breath. Sit, breathe, and just be, allowing yourself to exist in this space and experience gratitude for the gift of another day.

Set your timer for 8 minutes and free write on the changes you have experienced in your life since beginning this journal. Try your best not to edit or overthink it, but jot down whatever comes to mind—the changes, both big and small, you have noticed in your body, mind, heart, and life after completing fifty-six days of this journal. End your time with a final deep breath, celebrating yourself for completing these eight weeks.

Closing Thoughts

AS YOU COMPLETE THE LAST PAGES OF THIS JOURNAL, THE FINAL THOUGHT THAT I WANT TO LEAVE YOU WITH IS TO ALWAYS STRIVE FOR PROGRESS OVER PERFECTION.

I had the ability to wave a magic wand and grant one wish, it would be that after completing all fifty-six days of this journal, you would feel completely anxiety-free, living independently from your thoughts. But chances are, that's not the case—and that's okay.

Most likely, there will never be a final endpoint to this journey. Moving through and working with anxiety is like planting a tree. The work is never really done. You have to keep showing up every day and watering your tree and, in turn, the tree will grow, its leaves reaching the sky and its roots growing deep and wide.

This journal was designed to help you build a solid foundation for growth, evolution, and progress in the fight against anxiety. I hope it has helped you learn to exist independently of your anxiety and your thoughts, and that you now have the tools in your toolbox to continue your daily practice, honor your safe space within, and grow each day.

I am so excited for you to continue this journey, and I thank you from the deepest part of my heart for allowing me to lead you through the last eight weeks. I honor you and I celebrate you. I hope you do the same for yourself, as you are the one who did the work, showed up every day, and put your well-being first.

Congratulations!

ACKNOWLEDGMENTS

I have to start by thanking my family, who helped support me during the writing process of this journal. Specifically, my husband for being a great co-parent as I raised this book baby (and our actual babies), my mom for cheering me on and checking in on me each week, and Porkchop, Mila, and Poppy for giving me many reasons to smile while this book was created.

Second, I want to thank Daniela and Anja for being incredible friends and always celebrating the wins with me, and never letting self-doubt be a part of my life. I wake up every day grateful for women like you.

Third, my *Mindful in Minutes* community who have changed my life and allowed my dreams to turn into reality.

Finally, the Quarto team for taking a chance on me and letting me create what I have written on my heart.

ABOUT THE AUTHOR

Kelly Smith is the founder of Yoga for You, the host of the iTunes chart-topping meditation podcast *Mindful in Minutes* and its sister podcast *Meditation Mama,* and the author of *Mindful in Minutes: Meditation for the Modern Family.* She is an E-RYT 500, YACEP, and master trainer in meditation, yoga nidra, and restorative yoga. Her meditations and work have been featured in *Meditation Magazine,* Popsugar Fitness, ABC News, The Bump, Twin Cities Live, and the Lavendaire Lifestyle Podcast. She lives in Minneapolis with her family. You can find her on Instagram as @yogaforyouonline.

MEDITATION
for the MODERN
FAMILY

Over 100 Practices to Help Families Find
Peace, Calm, and Connection

KELLY SMITH

Host of the Mindful in Minutes Podcast

Also available by Kelly Smith

Mindful in Minutes: Meditation for the Modern Family

Over 100 Practices to Help Families Find Peace, Calm, and Connection

ISBN: 978-0-7603-8214-1

Slow down, calm down, and come together with this complete guide to meditation for the whole family—featuring targeted practices for parents, teens, and kids of all ages.

Mindful in Minutes: Meditation for the Modern Family helps families of all kinds learn how to use meditation to cope with the everyday struggles of being a person who is also part of a family. Covering topics ranging from quieting the mind and managing stress to handling resentment and cultivating compassion, this book offers specialized practices for each family member by age—adults, teens and older kids, and small children. Topics include:

Being Present	Burnout
Finding Joy	Insomnia
Anxiety	Self-Confidence
Hyperactivity	Overstimulation
Worthiness	Connecting with the True Self
Empathy	And much more

The book also includes a series of dedicated meditations for expectant parents, a series of meditations to promote a healthy, loving relationship between partners, and over 250 mantras to help you focus your mind and go deeper into your practice.

Quarto.com

First Published in 2024 by Fair Winds Press, an imprint of The Quarto Group,
100 Cummings Center, Suite 265-D, Beverly, MA 01915, USA.
T (978) 282-9590 F (978) 283-2742

Fair Winds Press titles are also available at discount for retail, wholesale, promotional, and bulk purchase. For details, contact the Special Sales Manager by email at specialsales@quarto.com or by mail at The Quarto Group, Attn: Special Sales Manager, 100 Cummings Center, Suite 265-D, Beverly, MA 01915, USA.

28 27 26 25 24   1 2 3 4 5

ISBN: 978-0-7603-8542-5

Digital edition published in 2024
eISBN: 978-0-7603-8543-2

Design: Tanya Jacobson
Illustration: Esté Hupp

Printed in China

The information in this book is for educational purposes only. It is not intended to replace the advice of a physician or medical practitioner. Please see your health-care provider before beginning any new health program.